WORLDWISE

ANCIENT ROME

Written by
Nick Pierce

Illustrated by
Andy Rowland

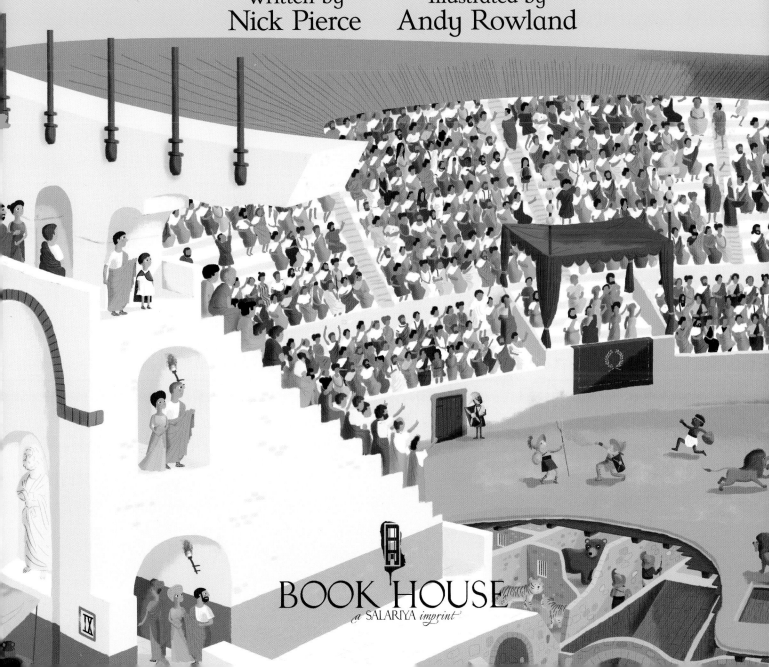

BOOK HOUSE
a SALARIYA *imprint*

This edition first published in MMXIX by
Book House

Distributed by Black Rabbit Books
P.O. Box 3263
Mankato, Minnesota 56002

Cataloging-in-Publication Data is available
from the Library of Congress

Printed in the United States
At Corporate Graphics,
North Mankato, Minnesota

9 8 7 6 5 4 3 2 1

ISBN: 978-1-912233-87-8

Contents

Introduction	4	Roman Schools	16
People of Rome	6	Roman Temples	18
Roman Soldiers	8	Timeline	20
Life In The City	10	Quiz	22
The Marketplace	12	Glossary	23
Entertainment	14	Index	24

Introduction

The Romans lived in Italy, more than 2,000 years ago. They began as farmers, but as they grew rich and powerful, they built a fine city, called Rome. Soon, they ruled the mightiest empire the world had ever seen. At its height, the Roman Empire covered about 30 of today's countries with about 50 million people living within its borders.

The city of Rome was the capital of the Roman Empire. It grew from tiny settlements and dates from around 800 BCE. In 64 CE, the city was devastated by fire, but was rebuilt and enlarged. In 271 CE a strong defensive wall was built around it. Almost a million people lived there in 50 BCE. Some were born in Rome, but many others came there, from the country, in search of work.

Roman civilization lasted for hundreds of years, from around 500 BCE to 400 CE. However, it did not disappear completely. Builders still used Roman designs. Engineers still relied on Roman technology. Today, we still use many Roman words.

On each spread you will have to look for different objects in the main picture.

People of Rome

R oman citizens believed that Rome was the best-run city in the world. It had good laws, fine buildings, fresh water, drains that worked, cheap entertainment, and free food for the poor. At first, Rome was ruled by kings. Then, in 509 BCE, it became a republic. It was ruled by officials who were chosen and voted for by the citizens. After 27 BCE, Rome was ruled by emperors. Some emperors were wise and fair; others were very bad.

▲Plebeians
Ordinary people were called "plebeians." They worked in shops, taverns, and market stalls, or were craftworkers.

1. Syrian

2. Numidian

3. Greek

4. Jew

◀People of the Empire
The Roman Empire included many different peoples:
1. Syrians 2. Numidians (North Africans) 3. Greeks 4. Jews.

◀Equites
Middle-ranking families were called "equites." They ran big businesses and owned buildings in the city of Rome.

▲Patricians
Rich families were called "patricians." They owned land in the country, and the men also had jobs as government officials.

▲Slaves
There were millions of slaves in Roman lands. They did the hardest, dirtiest work. They were owned by their master or mistress.

▶Soldiers
How many soldiers can you see?

▲Sandals
Soldiers could march up to 31 miles (50 kilometers) a day. They wore leather sandals.

▲Legionary
Legionaries agreed to serve in the army for 25 years. They were paid regular wages.

▲Helmet
How many helmets can you see in this picture?

Roman Soldiers

The Roman army was the best in the world. At first, the army was made up of ordinary citizens. It was led by officers called tribunes, and divided into legions of about 5,500 men. But, by around 100 BCE, the army was also recruiting soldiers from other lands who joined in order to travel and make money.

◄Digging soldiers
Can you find these soldiers?

◀Fighting soldiers
Can you find these soldiers training?

▲Armor
Soldiers covered their shoulders, back, and chest with armor made of linked metal strips.

Roads
Roman roads were built throughout the Empire so that the army could march quickly to trouble-spots. Most roads were planned and built by soldiers.

▲Cooking pot
A Roman soldier carried a cooking pot and three days' food rations with him. Basic rations were grain and salt, which soldiers cooked on camp fires to make porridge.

▶Tent
How many tents can you see in this picture?

9

Can you find...?

Life In The City

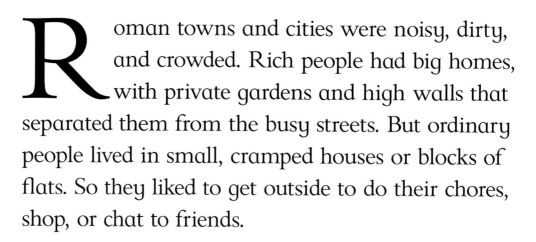

▲ Water fountain
Roman streets were paved with stone. There could be an open drain along one side, full of rubbish and smelly water. There were public lavatories and drinking-water fountains on many street corners.

R oman towns and cities were noisy, dirty, and crowded. Rich people had big homes, with private gardens and high walls that separated them from the busy streets. But ordinary people lived in small, cramped houses or blocks of flats. So they liked to get outside to do their chores, shop, or chat to friends.

▲ Insulae
Big blocks of apartments were called "insulae." There were shops at street level and small attics under the roof. The best rooms were on the first floor.

◀ Window
Can you find this boy looking out of a window?

◄Dog
Can you find this dog in the picture?

◄Baker
Can you find this baker in the picture?

▲Dangers
There were plenty of hazards in the narrow city streets. Robbers lurked. Rubbish was thrown out of windows overhead. Smelly drains, dung, rotting vegetables, and blood and guts from the butcher all needed to be avoided.

▲Traffic
In Rome, the streets got so crowded that no wheeled traffic was allowed during the day.

►Slaves
Can you find these slaves in the picture?

11

The Marketplace

Romans worked hard to earn a living. There were over 150 trades, from brewers and corn-dealers to wine merchants, dyers, chemists, cake-bakers, weavers, fishmongers, florists, boot-menders, wagon-drivers, and goldsmiths. There were thousands of small businesses too, like local taverns and barbers' shops. Ordinary citizens taught their children the skills they had as traders or craftworkers.

▲Manual work
Poor Romans never learned to read or write, so they had to work with their hands instead.

▲Carpenter
Boys from ordinary families were taught craft skills by their fathers.

▶Market stall
How many market stalls do you see in this picture?

◀Chickens
How many chickens can you count in this picture?

▲Transport
A packhorse, donkey, or mule was the cheapest form of transport for going short distances.

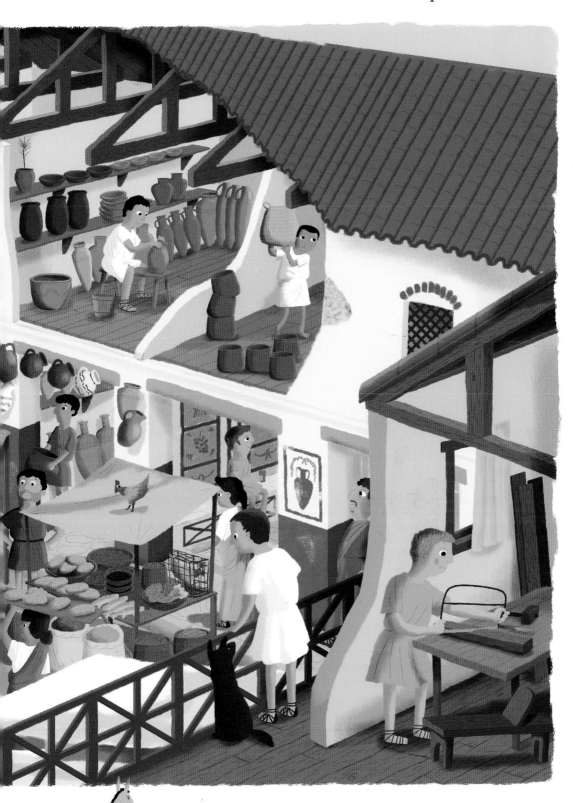

▲Potter
Skilled craftworkers, like this potter, could earn a good wage.

◀Cart
Oxen and donkeys pulled carts loaded with goods to and from the market.

▲Dog
Can you find the dog in this picture?

Can you find...?

▲Seating
The Colosseum in Rome, (built 80 CE) had 500,000 seats.

▲Bear
Can you find this bear in the picture?

▲Emperor
The emperor decided if a defeated gladiator should live or die.

Entertainment

Roman audiences enjoyed plays, music, and dancing. But the biggest crowds went to watch chariot races, or to see gladiators fight, or slaughter wild beasts. These animals were tormented to make them ferocious in the arena. Gladiators were often prisoners or slaves, forced to fight until they died. Charioteers and horses risked being killed each time they raced.

◀Bestiarius
Gladiators called "bestarii" fought wild animals like snakes, lions, and bears.

◀Lion
Can you find the lion in this picture?

▲Fighting
Gladiator contests were displays of strength and courage—qualities that were admired by the Romans.

▲Prisoners
Prisoners were held captive until it was time for them to be killed for the audience's entertainment.

▲Senators
The best seats were reserved for senators.

▶Gladiators
A few successful gladiators became rich and famous.

15

Roman Schools

Only boys from wealthy families went to school when they were 7 years old. They learned to read and write and to do sums. They went on to a higher level school when they were 12 to learn Roman history and to study poems by famous Greek and Roman writers.

Can you find...?

▲**Exercise**
Roman boys were also taught to keep fit. Schoolteachers said they should aim to have "a healthy mind in a healthy body."

▲**Public speaking**
Boys who wanted a career in government had to learn how to make speeches in front of large numbers of people.

17

Can you find...?

Roman Temples

The Romans worshipped many different gods and goddesses, each with special powers to guide or protect those people who prayed to them. Each god had his or her own temple, close to the Forum (marketplace).

▲ **Jupiter**
Jupiter was king of the gods. He controlled thunder and lightning.

▲ **Sacrifices**
At festivals animals might be killed as sacrifices. The Romans believed that animal sacrifices pleased the gods. These animals were killed at altars in front of the city's biggest temples.

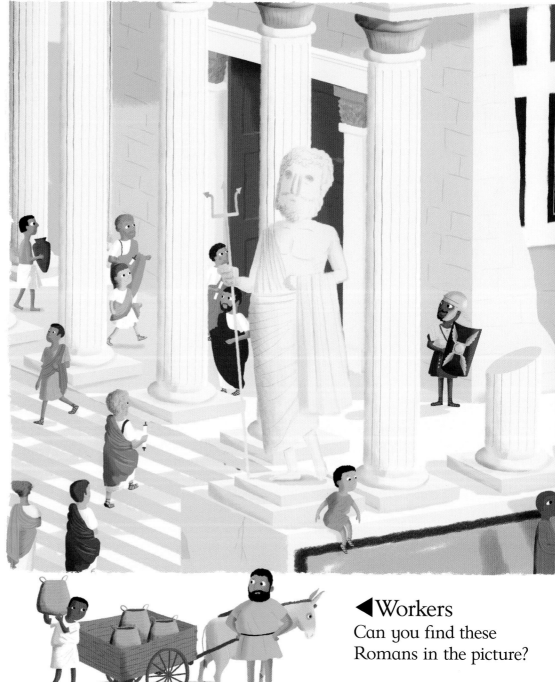

◀ **Workers**
Can you find these Romans in the picture?

▶Prayers

Every day, families said prayers to the "Lares" and "Penates," the gods who protected the household.

▼Fire

Can you find the fire in the picture?

▼Neptune

Neptune was god of the sea.

◀Priests

Temple priests and priestesses performed the sacrifices and religious ceremonies.

Timeline

753 BCE

The date traditionally given for the founding of Rome. The city grew from a group of villages on the seven hills beside the River Tiber.

58–44 BCE

Julius Caesar becomes Rome's greatest ruler. A group of senators who think he has become too powerful murder him in the Senate.

510–27 BCE

Rome emerges as the dominant power in the region. By 31 BCE, the whole of Italy and most of the countries around the Mediterranean have fallen to Rome.

27 BCE–14 CE

The Roman Empire is established. Augustus becomes Rome's first emperor. Peace reigns in Rome and the Empire grows overseas.

54–68 CE
The reign of Emperor Nero during which the Great Fire destroys two-thirds of Rome in 64 CE.

312–337 CE
Emperor Constantine founds the city of Constantinople (modern Istanbul). It becomes the capital of the Eastern Roman Empire. Christianity spreads throughout the Roman Empire.

69–80 CE
Emperor Vespasian orders the building of the Colosseum in Rome.

406–476 CE
The Western Empire of Rome is overrun by barbarian tribes and collapses. Rome is invaded and destroyed.

Quiz

1. How many millions of people once lived in the Roman Empire?

2. In what year did emperors start to rule over Rome?

3. Who planned and built most Roman roads?

4. What was the name for big blocks of apartments?

5. What name was given to a gladiator who fought wild animals?

6. Did all boys go to school?

7. Who was the king of the gods in Roman religion?

8. Why were animals part of religious ceremonies?

9. How many seats were in Rome's Colosseum?

10. How long did a legionary serve in the army?

Answers:

1. 50 million
2. 27 BCE
3. Roman soldiers
4. Insulae
5. Bestiarii
6. Only wealthy boys
7. Jupiter
8. They were sacrificed
9. 500,000
10. 25 years

Glossary

Armor Metal coverings worn to protect soldiers from harm during warfare.

Chariot A vehicle with two wheels that is pulled by horses.

Citizen Someone who lives in a city.

Emperor Strong ruler with total power.

Empire Lands ruled by a foreign power.

Gladiator Someone who fought and died to entertain Roman crowds.

Patrician Someone from a rich family.

Plebeian An ordinary person.

Republic Government by elected officials.

Senate Group of government officials in republican Rome.

Senator A member of the Senate.

Slave Someone who is owned by another person and must obey and work for them.

Index

A
animal sacrifices 18

C
Colosseum 14, 15, 21

E
emperors 6, 14, 20, 21, 23
equites 7

G
gladiators 14, 15, 23
gods 18, 19

I
insulae 10

J
Julius Caesar 20

M
market 6, 12, 13, 18

P
patricians 7, 23
plebeians 6, 23
priests 19
prisoners 14, 15

S
school 16, 17
slaves 7, 11, 14, 23
soldiers 7, 8, 9, 23